Rosy Cellophane: A book of writings inspired by a journey in search of love and understanding

Carol Walker Jordan

First Edition

ISBN 978-0-6151-4201-2

Cover Art:
Photos by David D. Jordan

Lulu Press
www.lulupress.com

For my family and friends who inspired me to look beyond what I read and what I see to find deeper meanings: David, Gideon, Jocelyn, Nick, Bill and all my beloved family and friends.

This book is for those people who may have walked my journey with me--in the parks, the gardens, the coffee shops, the libraries, the museums, the churches, and the streets of New York, Boston, Philadelphia, Chicago, Washington, DC, Seattle, Atlanta, Charleston, Columbia, Austin, New Orleans, St. Louis, Cincinnati, Kauai, Tel Aviv, Paris, Jerusalem, Charlottesville, Memphis, Nashville, San Francisco, Asheville and Charlotte.

Rosy Cellophane

A book of writings inspired by a journey in search of love and understanding.

PART ONE: ON STAGE

Actors

Beautiful bodies and magical eyes pull us
inside their web
Voices sweet and lyrical, harsh or quizzical
Touch our secret places and open us to
vulnerable attachments

Faces accentuated with paint and powder
Ask us to suspend disbelief
Hands and fingers moving, pointing,
snapping, clapping or shaking
Bring linguistic messages and send energy
shooting outward

Feet beguiling, frenzied or erotic
Promise us joy and freedom
Upon these shoulders rests the explication
of Life's joys, ironies, agonies, and tragedies

Rosy Cellophane

Taking our weariness with life as we know it
and making the days of our journey
beautiful

The Mime

No voice
A face
Two hands

Stark white face
Soft white gloves
Black clothes

Still and silent
Movement and joy
Harmony and mystery

Closeted in a world of silence
Doomed to no oral purpose
Endowed with body language
The Mime captures our hearts

The Trio

Night falls
Sidewalks glisten
Shops glow amber in the lights
A trio in the familiar

Music sweet and syncopated
Dancers quick and lithe
Cuisine delicate and tempting
A trio of seduction

On the stage he speaks of tragedy
In the audience, a woman cries
Behind the curtain, a director stands silent
A trio living in the moment

Morning comes
Evening stars fade

Sounds of the city rise
A trio of renewal

PART TWO: MAGIC

Blithe and Lively Lovely One

The light falls round him like a mantle
He sleeps oblivious to its warmth
It is the early rays of morning
And his dreams are far away

Somewhere outside he hears a sound
He remembers the ducks on the pond
When he gets around to it
He'll chase them 'til they fly

Cockatiels

Cockatiels travel in pairs
White snowy feathers
Orange cheeks
Two toes fore and two toes aft
Ethereal creatures cloaked in pure raiment
Piercing black eyes
Aware of their predators, cockatiels strut
their beauty cautiously
Knowing they may glisten only against the
white sands of the beach

Cockatiels seek anonymity
Aware of their beauty and vulnerability
Seeking to live, love and contribute
Cockatiels guard themselves
Living a life within the backdrop of a white
mandate

Coot

Shiny black feathers
Short yellow bill
Now you see him, now you don't
Submerged for an instant
He reappears and quacks his victory

Fluid movements on the water
Oblivious to weather
Invisible at night
Ceaseless searching
For what lies beneath
A coot finds his meal
One dive at a time

Eager to try his luck
With the ducks and geese
He raises himself
Flaps his wings and attempts to fly

Skipping across the water

He comes to rest a few feet from where he

started

Coots are like us

In endless pursuit of

Our daily bread

We go through each day

With a predictable rhythm

Yet when we try to fly

Our bodies are so heavy

We cannot lift off

The Feral Cat

Outside my window
A mound of yellow fur
Sits lazily on the ledge

Content to soak in the morning sun
With purrs like a roar of rapids
Acquainted with his kingdom
He pretends to sleep

Born under the floor boards
To a family of six
All gone now
Alert to nothing it seems
He knows no fear
He is king of the campus green

Assured of a full bowl
Confident of unconditional love

His only weakness

The unexpected days

When loneliness reigns

PART THREE:
OBSERVATIONS

Adventures

Trying to stretch beyond the present
Looking for ways to add zest and fun to life as
she knows it
Hoping for intellectual challenge and new
relationships
The woman sprints along a path
Whose dangers she knows quite well

To hold a steady course
To build a rock solid foundation
To establish a predictable table of security
The woman squirms and wiggles
She knows no joy or exhilaration from
sameness

Curiosity killed the cat
Her father warned
Nothing ventured, nothing gained
Her mother murmured

Try your idea and ask for permission later
Her mentor challenged

Where does the drive to go beyond the expected
originate?
Why do some of us find ourselves victims of
this passion?
How do others of us cast it aside?
What do the brave hearted possess that the
faint hearted know to ignore?
Like a rocket set to shoot beyond the stars, she
knows there is a point of no return
But she drinks the fuel of the moment and flies
off to parts unknown

The Amethyst

Deep purple

Rich and enchanting

The color of a Queen's robe

Mounted in a silver base

Given in love and devotion

On a birthday

Called the "Addicts Stone"

Intended to lessen unwanted habits

Release addictions

Enhance peace, intuition and balance

Was this gift given in hopes of encouraging

Strength in the face of adversity?

Did he know of her psychic abilities?

Would the amethyst

Worn on the middle finger of her right hand

Enhance her ability to see the vision

She so desperately seeks?

Will the deep purple gemstone change her life?

Beware the Disingenuous

He comes into the room
Smiling with out-stretched hand
Speech so fluid it drips from his lips
Eyes so fixed
He captures his victim

Day after day
Year after year
He makes his way by conquering
All those who cross his path
And all those whom he seeks to know

One day someone asks
What did he say?
What does he stand for?
How often does he do as he says?
Suspicions rise

The wise ones

Caution allegiance to the man

Without substance

Caution inclusion based upon words alone

Recommend embracing when truth is

substantiated

Classrooms and Life on the Street

The scent is of old wood and chalkboards
The windows from floor to ceiling
boast many unwashed panes
Stickers and construction paper dot walls
Pencil sharpeners make cranky sounds
As children prepare for class

Tables and chairs in a semi-circle
No more desks bolted to the floor in rows
Student teams energized by diversity
No more white bread of the same grains
No sitting quietly and copying
Shouting, interrupting, challenging, and
pushing
Today's children reflect life on the street

Classroom management
Teachers cry for help

Where do I begin today's lessons?
The voice is an ineffectual tool
Hoarseness claims the throat at day's end
Only the television screen attached to the
ceiling
The video designed to imitate life on the
street
Brings order to the madness and stills the
chaos

Hooligans

Some declare they are Irish,
Other swear they are German,
My mother is determined they are "the little
people"
Our next door neighbor points to the
Hispanic grocer
Determined he looks suspicious

The trash cans are turned over
Car windows are smashed
Walls are spray painted with graffiti
Sidewalks are smeared with the remains of
someone's dinner
Who are these hooligans?

Hooligans are rarely the Irish neighbors
Or the German neighbors
Or the "little people"

Or the Hispanic grocer

Hooligans are people who have never

learned to love themselves

Shiny Black Cabriolets

The sounds of horses' hooves ring through
dark streets
Dogs and children jump to the sidewalks
Taking their stick balls with them
Bystanders turn to see who passes
At such a frantic pace

Shiny black cabriolets, two by two,
Race by the onlookers
Where are they headed?
What is their mission?
Inside the cabriolets

Shielded by the drawn curtains
Four men prepare last minute defense
tactics for an afternoon murder trial
When the cabriolets stop and the
passengers depart,

Will they be able to keep up with the paperwork?

PART FOUR: INSPIRATION

Aphrodisiac

What did you say?
Oysters, yuk!
Chocolate, yum!
Red wine? I doubt it
Milk No way
Flowers, maybe

The sound of a voice
The scent of a body,
The chords of a familiar song,
Words oft repeated appearing in a
daydream

Aphrodisiacs
Call us to touch and feel
A treasure we keep hidden deep inside
Buried for fear of pain and loss
So tempting and so terrifying

Dreams

Do you ever dream in Technicolor?
Colors so bright your eyes are burning?
Light so intense you want to wake up?

Are your dreams filled with anxiety?
Filled with dragons, weapons, fire, and
torment?
Pressure so great you awake in a fright?

Is your dream the same night after night?
Are the same people in your dreams?
Do they seem so out of place and without
form?

Are you in a house? A car? On a boat?
Are you traveling so fast that your clothes
are blowing in the wind?

Is someone calling to you?

Are you climbing a tree?
Making love by an open fire?
Washing your hair?

Dreams tell us of the moment or of the
distant past
Dreams encapsulate our frustrations and our
joys
Hiding meanings from us until we tell them to
others

Family

Living, breathing, union
Connected by a magical substance in the
veins
Members by blood

Matriarchy, patriarchy
Matri-lineage, patri-lineage
Man, woman, child

Family defined through blood
What of
The childless couple?

The widow and a stepson?
A child, orphaned at birth?
An old man, with no living relatives?

Family begins in blood

Family extends beyond blood

Family lives in shared lives

Ficus, Flowers, Tic Tac Toe

The pious Ficus, silent and still
Stretches for the light of early morning

Flowers, scented and colorful
Permanent yet fading speak of love

Tic Tac Toe, beautiful and tiny
Painted faces of clay on a marble board

What makes a house a home
A Ficus, a flower and a board game?

Guardian Angels

A child runs to catch his dog

A pilot finds himself flying into a storm

A horse tries to jump a barbed wire fence

A lamb is separated from her mother

A teacher is confronted by a student with a
gun

A grandmother opens her door to a
stranger

A deer drinks from a polluted stream

A goose eats grass treated with insecticide

An acrobat feels his cable snap

A sailor is thrown overboard

A woman is raped

A man learns he is HIV positive

Children, pilots, horses, and lambs
Teachers, grandmothers, deer, and geese
Acrobats, sailors, women, and men
Need guardian angels

Hearts and Flowers

Climbing the porch and trailing along the
plank floor
The ivy seeks new paths
Hanging from the ceiling on eye-hooks
The swing moves silently in the breeze

All is still in the noon day sun
Except for the saw blades of the
grasshoppers
Who bask and bake and wait

Summer in the south
Softens the hearts
Slows the pace
Turns thoughts to hearts and flowers
Trying to understand

"You cannot motivate a satisfied man"
The words were clearly spoken
Why were these words so profound to her?
Why did they rivet her heart?

He said his goal is to be,
To walk through endless days,
To eat, drink, sleep, and breathe,
Simple ways
Filled with mornings, afternoons and night

He said he is satisfied
Life is good
Time is his to use as he pleases
He wants for nothing
As his basic needs are
Given by her for his pleasure

She doesn't understand
Why is enough all he wants?
Why doesn't he hear a small voice inside
Calling him to stretch and reach beyond
himself?

She hears that voice
Why is it absent in him?

Hill Dwellers

Mountain people live in the valleys
On the sides of hills
At the base of the mountain
Beside a stream that runs down the
mountain
Confident in their oneness with nature's
spirits
To be in and of the mountain
To be one with the mountain is ethereal

Who would live on the top of a mountain
Only a fool
Winter winds blast the tops of the
mountains
Snow covers paths and roads
Rain and lightning bolts assault the ridges
Streams run down not up

Hill Dwellers look down

Mountain people look up and around

Nature gives them meaning for life

Hill Dwellers invade the temples of the

spirits

Desecrating the sacred ridges with their

bricks and mortar

Jazzy Starbucks

Atop her head sits a tiara
Atop the tiara is a star
Long wavy hair flows around her shoulders
and curvy sides
With deep set eyes, she flirts and hides her
charms

In a place where celestial imaginings come
easily
A place for random thoughts
Alone or with a crowd
Community abounds

Wide plank floors
A fireplace
Bistro tables, mismatched chairs,
newspapers, magazines

Slouchy sofas under track lights

Everywhere the aroma, sights and sounds
Of café au lait, café mocha, steamed milk
and white chocolate,
From Seattle to Boston to Philadelphia to
Charlotte to Atlanta
Jazzy Starbucks has her way

Kitty Hawk

Dunes so high they reach the sky
Sand so white it dazzles the eye
Breezes so strong they lift and pitch
Twist and turn our handmade kites

Quiet, secluded, jutting into the Atlantic
Kitty Hawk once seduced
Two brothers determined to fly
A wooden and canvas bird

Climbing the dunes
Running along the beaches
Watching and feeling the air currents
The two walked the beach for hours

Quarreling and arguing,
Dragging their makeshift bird

Rosy Cellophane

Two brothers dreamed the impossible
And Kitty Hawk complied

Live for Today

When countless days have passed

Which one will be remembered?

The day we waited for

Or the day we lived serendipitously

Lyrics from Dead People

Frank Sinatra?
Patsy Cline?
How easily the mind brings their voices
alive
Inside our heads

Connecting the day, the time, the mood
When we first heard those voices
Chain us to their lyrics
Recurring inside our heads

Why does a song live on?
Why do certain voices capture and control
our moods?
Is their legacy the lyrics
Recycling through our heads?

Dead people are ever alive

Passing from one eternity to another

Imbedded in the beauties or tragedies of life

Through their lyrics within our heads

Music

Sweet stirrings in the soul
Reminiscent of feelings
Hidden deep within
Crying for escape
Knowing no sure path

Touching places where no one goes
Except in moments totally unguarded
Like a knife in sweet butter
Silent and sure
Riveting the senses and blocking intuition

Jolting the moment
Spreading like volcanic ash
Tumbling to its destination
Swift and smothering
Disabling the most mighty

Music of the heart

Finds our deepest longings

Quiets our raging emotions

Stampedes our cautions

Elevates our dreams

Open Your Hand and Let It Fly

The fingers close securely
Around the polished stone
There is no danger of loss
Her heart is not alone

The magician touches her hand
The stone is turned to life
Inside the tightly held spirit
Struggles and cries for sight

To open her fingers means loss
The heart will suffer the pain
No longer her secret treasure safe in her
hand
Close by and easily seen

The fingers slowly open
Tears begin to fall

The life flows forth and flies away
The fingers touch it as it goes

Pocket Watch

Climbing onto the platform of the train
Signaling to the engineer to start the engine
Shoveling the coal to keep the fire going
Day in and day out, year after year
Hoping for the watch

Do your job with a pure heart
Treat everyone as an equal
No work is dishonorable if done by an
honorable man
Work overtime, never take vacations
Sure to get the watch

Forty years of hard work
The day comes and the watch is awarded
He admires it lovingly, attaches it to his vest
Arranges the gold chain so that it glints in
the sunlight

The watch is his

Swinging from the gold chain
The watch they gave him for forty years of
service
Bent, broken, hands swollen, eyes dimmed
He dresses each morning and attaches the
gold chain
And the watch

Ribbons

A rainbow is filled with ribbons
Crayons are ribbons in disguise
School children in the Bronx are ribbons in
the rough
Grunge music is a collection of frayed
ribbons
New plays are emerging ribbons, yet to be
colored

Silky, a delight to the beholder
A treasure to mark the pages of a work
Grained, decorated, sequined and tied into
complex designs
Ribbons invigorate our passions
For beauty, diversity, togetherness and
perfection

Serendipity

She sits and watches
The morning mist rises over the water
The Blue Crane stands as sentinel to the
sun
The sounds of traffic begin to build
And a crescendo of activity is in motion

She asks
Where does the silence go?
How do the droplets from the mist
disappear?
What happens to the quiet and unseen?
Why must silence exist in contrast to
activity?

She knows
The woman in her sadness knows no silence
The world is internal, swirling and burning

There is no comfort in activity
Her life is not her own

She waits
Caught in the world of the unseen
She moves and sits and stops
Ever vigilant for the peace
She so desperately would find

Shadows

Sun and moon are the mother and father
Shadows awake and come to life
As the sun rises
Shadows walk softly and come to bed
As the Moon makes its way across the sky

A lone figure walks upon the beach by
morning light
In front of him glides a shadowy friend
When he returns home at day's end
The shadowy friend follows closely behind

Who is the shadowy friend?
He is beauty in silence
Comfort in constancy
Playful in different lights
Appropriately respectful
Engagingly playful

A reflection of what goes before or comes
behind

Life is rich with shadowy friends
Who reflect the image we project
Shadowy friends are of us and apart from
us
We are the genesis of their being
We are the recipients of their grace

Tears

They come when we're born
They come when we love
They come when we're happy
They come when we part
They come when we fear

Birth, love, happiness, loss and danger
Life's promises to the fragile

They come when we can't express our
feelings
They come when we experience the pain of
others
They come when we walk in a strong wind
They come when we remember
They come when we hear

Our hearts, our souls and our bodies
Find release and renewal in our tears

Tears are gifts from guardian angels to
remind us
We are capable of being divine

The Alabaster Box

Secret thoughts need places to live
Secret dreams need safety and protection to
grow
Secret fears need openings to escape
An alabaster box holds her secret thoughts,
dreams and fears

Human spirits long for a place ethereal
Past lives crowd the integrity of the
moment
Elusive to the eye
Real to the emotion
Where is the dwelling she seeks?

A simple alabaster box
So fragile, so exquisite
Offers a safe house

For silent thoughts, wistful dreams
And misgivings

Three AM

All is still and quiet under the black sky
Across the streets, shops and houses,
Tiny points of light twinkle
No traffic moves and sirens are stilled

On a street corner a dimly lighted shop
front
Reveals a collection of small tables and
stools
The aroma of bread and sweet rolls
Wafting upward invades the early morning
air
A cat is curled patiently on the doormat
Waiting for a sign of welcome
And her dish of sweet cream

Above the street in a small sitting room
A writer finds richness in the view below

Shades of night unleash the spirit of

Morpheus

But rest and slumber she knows not

Her craft drives her Three A M engagement

Three AM is a time for wonder

Three AM is a space for reflection

Three AM lifts a writer's intuition

Three AM passes too quickly

The beauty of Three AM to a writer

Is the joy found in solitude

Time to Reflect

They sit in rocking chairs and stare in
silence
It is the time in life that they thought would
bring
Lovely sweet mornings and beautiful
sunsets
A time when they would finally be carefree
A time when life would be the culmination
of their dreams

They sit in rocking chairs and stare
Around them the voices are incoherent
The behaviors are strange and bizarre
The smells are not pleasant
The food is unappealing

They sit in rocking chairs
The hours go by

And they do not notice
Up close they hear the clock ticking
The time for reflection is here
Yet the mind has gone to rest

Tiny Confetti Hearts

Sprinkled inside the pages of a note
Carrying messages
Of love and mystery
Tiny confetti hearts spill before us
As the words appear

Hidden inside a tissue
Scented with lavender and placed in a cedar
drawer
Tiny confetti hearts bring a smile
As they stick to the fingers and sparkle in
the light

Dropped in a chain across the floor
Winding throughout the room
Going up a stair
Trailing out a window sill

Rosy Cellophane

Tiny confetti hearts buoy our spirits
Make us laugh with thoughts of love

Tumbleweeds

Their paths are never known
Each moment of motion is unrehearsed
The lift of the moment
Gives them flight

They gallop into town
Swirl at the local bar
Pick up a dollar in a poker game
Drink a pint of scotch

From above the angels look down
Upon these free and carefree men
Who take the high road
Knowing nothing of the angels' envy

PART FIVE: JOY

Latte and Beignets

All black and white linens
Tiny violets in translucent cylinders
French spoken here
Between tiny tables
Cabaret singers and blues men compete
Jugglers and soft-shoe artists dance
Life is good

It's five o'clock in the French Quarter
Life is beginning
Café au lait
Appear in old white ceramic cups and
saucers
The powdery confections arrive
Life is good

Waiters, sitting along a wall

Joie de vivre hair, wedged to fall over one

eye

Heads tilted in anticipation

Expect a request for service

Evening falls on Café du Monde

Life is good

Lemon Meringues at 4 o'clock

Tucked invitingly behind a massive urn of
lilies of the valley,
A grand piano and a tea cart
Small tables and tapestry-covered chairs
Invite weary travelers to 4 o'clock tea

In this seaport town touted for its elegant
cuisine,
Charleston's Charleston Place
Comes alive at 4 o'clock
The pianist arrives
Porcelain tea cups and Irish linen are
arranged
Voices are lowered
Tea is poured

The pastry cart rolls noiselessly through the
room

Amid the

Scones

Iced cakes

Cucumber sandwiches

Cheese straws

Strawberries dipped in white

chocolate

The specialty of the day rises on a tall cake

stand

The specialty is Lemon Meringues

Everyday at 4 o'clock

The pastry cart rolls past

Refreshed and entranced travelers

Who drink tea,

And consume pastries,

Turn to each other and say

"Let's stay another day and see tomorrow's

specialty"

Marmalade Toast

Children like apple jelly toast
Old men want grape jelly toast
Country cousins want apple butter toast
Who wants marmalade toast?

It's bittersweet
It's full of peel
It's has a funny name
Who would ever want marmalade toast?

Was it Babar? Curious George?
The Man with the Yellow Hat?
Was it Madeline? Big Bird? Ms Frizzle?
Could it have been Christopher Robin?
Who wanted marmalade toast?

Grandmothers!
Grandmothers love marmalade

Tea and toast and marmalade

Irish tea cups and linen napkins

The passing of the love of marmalade

The Patio

Hot bricks and cool wrought iron
Hidden under an umbrella of green
A waiter with a white apron
Crusty bread, oil and balsamic vinegar
Mingle in the sun at noon

Smiles and tales of friends and foes
Talk of scenes so absurd
The meek and mild fear the malevolent
beasts
The strong and clever declare them but
headless wonders

Bottled water no ice
Salads no onions
Pizza no anchovies
Smiles no tears
Life on a summer's day—Nirvana on a patio

Uptown Sunday

The sun drives home its joy
Creating dazzling reflections in the glass
fronts of the skyscrapers
Warm breezes slip about the corners
Roughing the waters in strategically placed
fountains
In uptown on Sunday

Restaurants open their doors
Spreading into the street with tables and
chairs
White tablecloths flap in the breeze
Conversations bounce back and forth as
waiters strain to hear
In uptown on Sunday

Ri Ra's serves beer, corned beef and
cabbage

The Capital Grille serves anything you want
a la' carte
Rock Bottom Brewery serves a grilled
chicken salad
The Dunhill serves a southern medley
Dixie's serves Creole
In uptown on Sunday

Repertory patrons press into the lobby of
the tall glass tower
Not sure what the afternoon holds
Dressed in loose comfortable clothes
The Sunday crowd is unpretentious
Psycopathia Sexualis: theatre at the Booth
In uptown on Sunday

PART SIX: HOPE

Bluebells

Alongside the low hills
Grow the gentle and fragile Bluebells
Wildflowers growing indiscriminately
Needing no help from human hands
Governed only by the gifts of nature

The eye is drawn to the Bluebell
The finger wants to touch
The sense of smell becomes alert
The hand wants to hold
The cobalt blue field flower

See, touch, smell, hold
Wrap oneself in beauty
For a moment the world disappears
The ethereal is real
Sitting in a field of Bluebells

Choppy Waters

The sun rises slowly
Welcome light floods the room
Chilly spring winds rattle the awning over
the deck
On the pond the water jumps
Hops and laps the walkway

Deep in the pond the fish stay close to the
bottom
Enjoying the warmth accumulated from
past days
Across the pond coots dive deeper than
usual
Determined to capture the breakfast they
found so easily
The warm day before

Hope

Choppy waters challenge the wise and the
determined
Calling us to seek safe spaces
Forcing us to expend more effort than we
might
Informing us of our vulnerability
Should we choose to ignore the challenge to
change

Cinders at Midnight

Half past midnight
A pounding at the door
Pulled from warm beds
Hustled into the dark night
Shadowy figures stand cold and
disbelieving
In a parking lot

Dark except for a wildly raging fire
Burning so fast
Spewing cinders and smoke
Challenging firefighters
To use their best training
While neighbors search for comfort
In hushed conversations

A hundred people in pajamas
Robes, sweatshirts, coats, tennis shoes

Hope

Braving the cold
Afraid with each crackle of the blaze
That the sparks and the wind will
Ignite their homes and their possessions

St Elmo's Fire, the Burning Bush
Fires of the Southwest
Fires in New York tenements
Fires in lava flows
Somehow so distant but now so close
In a parking lot just past midnight

Clover Blossoms

What beauty abounds in a patch of clover
blossoms
Lovely and rich the mood is fun and invites
the bare feet to dance
Yet the secret of the clover blossom is well
hidden
Beneath the beauty is a treacherous beast
Armed with a secret weapon the clover
blossom knows its defender

The happy hum of the fat furry bee adds
music to the allure of the clover blossom
How can this beautiful scene be filled with
danger
What lurks there to punish the intruder?
Is it always what we see that informs our
decisions?
What must we explore before we place our

summer feet into the clover patch?

Beauty perceived is beauty beheld
Beauty understood is beauty informed
Clover blossoms ask us to take the beauty
of the moment with caution
Hold it with tenderness
And venture no farther than we are
prepared to go

Ferns and Lichens

Deep within the Appalachian woods,
Lies a mystical garden without a gardener
A serene and quiet place
Created by nature
And left to evolve as symbiosis sets the lead

A tiny trail made smooth by many feet
Bare feet, moccasin feet, trail boot feet,
No campsites and no benches
No wheels of any kind
Lovers walk by and marvel as symbiosis
sets the lead

Clear and cold water passes down the
stream
Ferns and lichens grow indiscriminately
Rock pools are sanctuaries to tiny fishes
Tall trees shade and filter the sun shafts

Hope

Invading to bring warmth and light
Deep within the Appalachian woods,
symbiosis sets the lead

Fireflies

Up into the summer night
Tiny points of yellow light
On and off
On and off

Lightning bugs
Mimosa trees
Mint Juleps
Straw hats

Deep within the summer grass
He calls to her
Come to me
Follow me

With the fading of the night
No more the points of light

Hope

Off and gone
Off and gone

Rosy Cellophane

Give Me A Window

If I have to live here, give me a window
Wash it and polish it and keep it free of
blind and shade
Let it be my window on the world
Let me watch the world go by
Let me see the way others live

Know that the chains that bind me
Are imaginary
That the house in which I dwell is no prison
But held here by the wishes of another
Whose feelings I much revere

If I have to live here, give me a mirror
For my reflection
Let me examine my eyes
Let me look deep to find understanding

Hope

Let me come to know why I feel imprisoned
By the space in which I live

Grey Skies and Bare Trees

Evening arrives, quiet settles
Car lights flicker passing below her
Grey misty skies backdrop a stand of wintry
bare trees
A lone horn delivers a message
Life moves and she watches

Imagination is alive
Watermelons, dandelions, honeybees and
hot sand beneath her feet
Peach blossom festivals, apple chill fairs
Sidewalk cafes and club sandwiches at
midnight
Life moves and she remembers

Music beckons her, soft light from candles
glowing
Silk pajamas and Paloma

Hope

Quiet introspective music, anticipation is
pervasive
Life moves and she lives in the moment

Love and a Willow

Some say the tap roots of a willow run deep
As the branches grow
Some say the tap roots of a love run deep
As the bonds grow strong
Deep and long; deep and strong
Willows and love are real and ethereal

A willow flourishes with abundant rain
A love flourishes with abundant nurture
A willow is beautiful and fragile
A love is beautiful and fragile
Beauty and fragility
Become wisdom and strength

Some say a willow only survives by a stream
of water
Some say a love only survives if there is

Hope

An ongoing source of caring

Willows and love
Real and ethereal
Beautiful and fragile
Wisdom and strength
Engenders a balance
Between nature and nurture

Moonlight

The pond sparkles in the moonlight
Ripples flap against the sides of the
walkway
Water black as the asphalt street
Hides the creatures that lurk underneath

Lights hidden in lamplight covers
Dimly illuminate the walkway
Giving lovers a romantic path
Hiding indiscretions from view

Clouds pass over and the moonlight
disappears
The black water blends with the darkened
grass and shrubs
Somewhere love is consummated
The moon reappears happy that its work is
done

My Garden

A truck garden, a rock garden, an herb
garden, a kitchen garden, a flower garden
None of these is like my garden
In my garden grow words
A word garden

Planted years ago with the most minimal of
words
Enriched as days went by with more exotic
plantings
Weeded on occasion as usefulness
diminished
Plowed under from time to time by life's
circumstances

My word garden lifts my spirits and
enlivens my thoughts
On some days it teaches me to be humble

and meek
Or it challenges me to dig deep to see if a
treasure is buried
Beneath the layers I have created

From morning to evening I call upon my
garden
Asking for help as I form my opinions,
impressions and feelings
Desperately attempting to describe the
workings of my mind and heart
On occasion, my garden is no help
It comes up short when I mention love; it
does not recognize this word

Rosy Cellophane

Frosty branches and skaters in the park
Steamed milk, mittens and cashmere
scarves
Warm the children against the cold

While on the streets' metal grates, the bag
lady sits
Shivering in the cold, looking up
To the penthouse suite
Where all is rosy cellophane

The pendulum swings
The bag lady whispers,
There but for the grace of God go I

Rosy, rosy cellophane
Rosy, rosy cellophane
Celebrate the joy of living
Celebrate the joy of giving

Sweet and Low

Cold wind slips around the alleys
Tall buildings erase the sun
Small storefronts promise comfort
Church spires beckon the devout

Loud and raucous in the street
Buses and trucks honk for attention
Loud and raucous beside the curb
Cabdrivers yell obscenities
Loud and raucous in the traffic
Fire trucks, police cars and emergency
vehicles
Scream their warnings

Sweet and low
Somewhere musicians play
Sweet and low
Somewhere lovers whisper

Hope

Sweet and low
Somewhere children laugh
Sweet and low

A city is loud and raucous
A city is sweet and low
Its energy is in its muscle
Its beauty is in its soul

Symphony of a City

Birds in a row on a roof top
Company in numbers
Children on a rope crossing a street
Safety in holding on

A lone traveler making his way through a
crowd
Gathers energy from the pace of the street
A solitary musician playing in a subway
station
Surrounds himself with music
An actor on a stage before the lights
Captures each moment of applause
A bag lady occupying her street corner
Sits with her treasures before her

Independent, brave, resilient, and
passionate

Hope

Bound by the commonality of city life
Birds, children, travelers, musicians, actors
and bag ladies
Find meaning in the symphony of a city

The Black Ribbon As Queen Bee

The hum is constant
The tone changes very little
Engines not so far away sound like bees
Making honey

Houses, apartments and condominiums
Built too close to the Interstate
Provide a sounding board
For the droning

The black ribbon stretches for miles
Invading and creating neighborhoods
The allure of constant movement
The magic of the Queen Bee

At two am the persistence of the hum
Annoys the sleepless writer
Where is my once peaceful neighborhood

Hope

Quiet, dark, serene and still?

Is there to be no rest near the relentless

Queen Bee?

Walden

A pen in a hand
Reveals a private self
Ink on a page releases
Bonds of silence

As words rise from the page
Eyes watch in wonder
As thoughts once scrambled
Form truths

Forbidden from living in the city
Welcomed to live in the woods
A pen and a paper
As constant companions
He practices his art in solitude
Comforted by truths his handwork reveals